Mom, Remember When . . .

A Treasury of Loving Reflections

Annie Pigeon

P

PINNACLE BOOKS

http://www.pinnaclebooks.com

PINNACLE BOOKS are published by

Kensington Publishing Corp.
850 Third Avenue
New York, NY 10022

Pinnacle and the P logo Reg. U.S. Pat. & TM Off.

First Printing: April, 1997
10 9 8 7 6 5 4 3 2 1

Printed in the United States of America

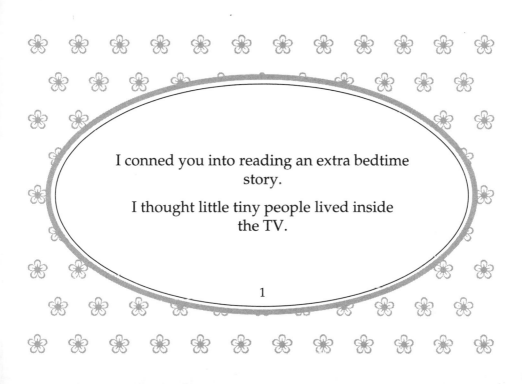

I conned you into reading an extra bedtime story.

I thought little tiny people lived inside the TV.

1

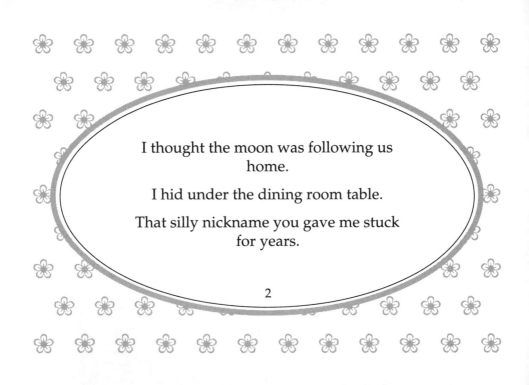

I thought the moon was following us home.

I hid under the dining room table.

That silly nickname you gave me stuck for years.

2

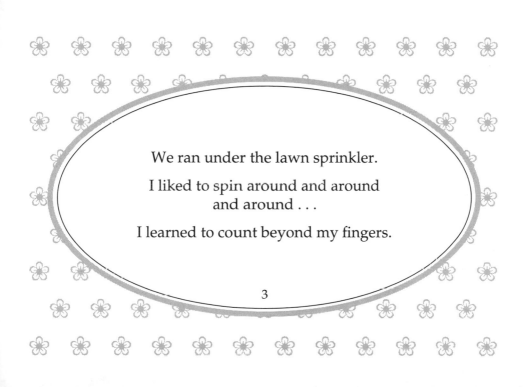

We ran under the lawn sprinkler.

I liked to spin around and around
and around . . .

I learned to count beyond my fingers.

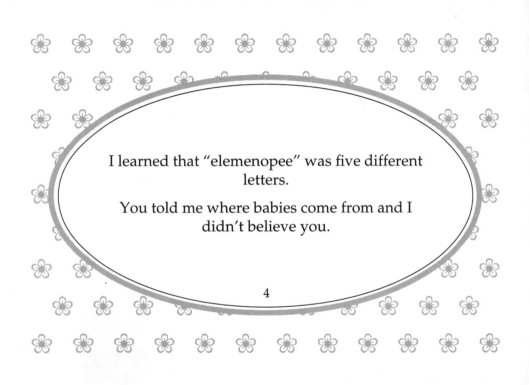

I learned that "elemenopee" was five different letters.

You told me where babies come from and I didn't believe you.

4

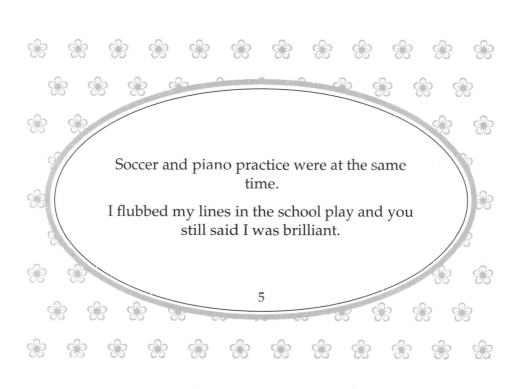

Soccer and piano practice were at the same time.

I flubbed my lines in the school play and you still said I was brilliant.

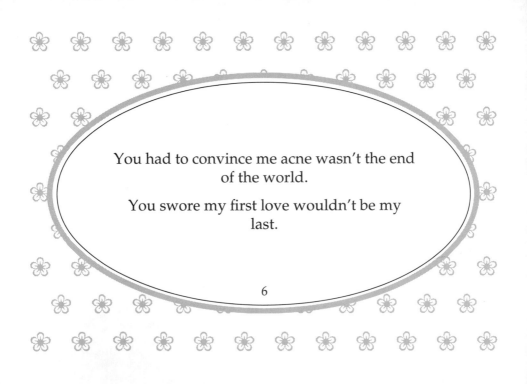

You had to convince me acne wasn't the end of the world.

You swore my first love wouldn't be my last.

You swore my baby fat wouldn't last forever.

I ate more syrup than pancakes.

I caught you and Dad kissing.

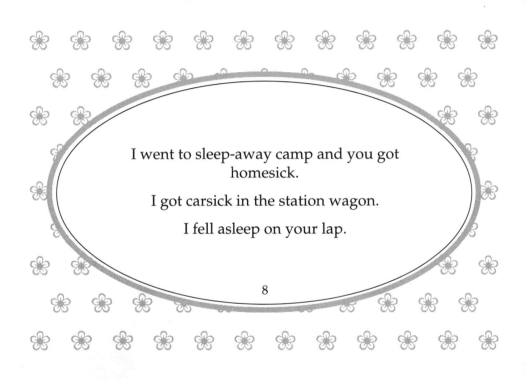

I went to sleep-away camp and you got homesick.

I got carsick in the station wagon.

I fell asleep on your lap.

8

I used to beg to help with household chores.

I thought I was rich if my piggy bank rattled.

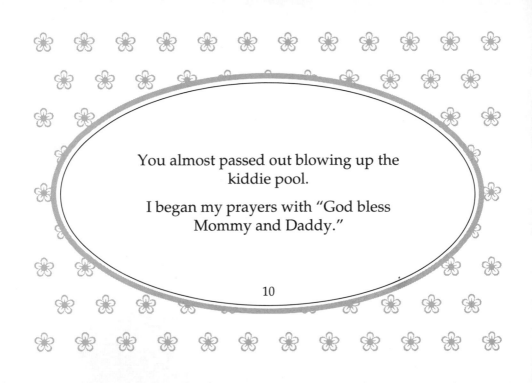

You almost passed out blowing up the kiddie pool.

I began my prayers with "God bless Mommy and Daddy."

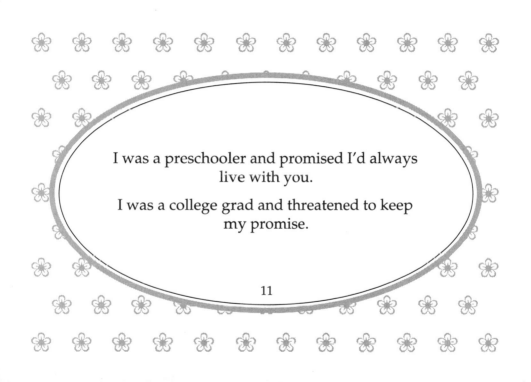

I was a preschooler and promised I'd always live with you.

I was a college grad and threatened to keep my promise.

11

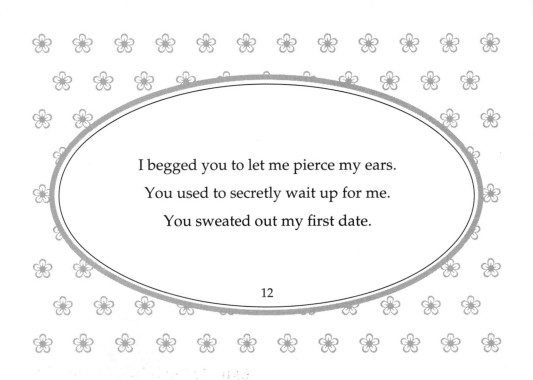

I begged you to let me pierce my ears.

You used to secretly wait up for me.

You sweated out my first date.

12

I took baths with rubber duckies.

You braided my hair.

We had tea parties.

13

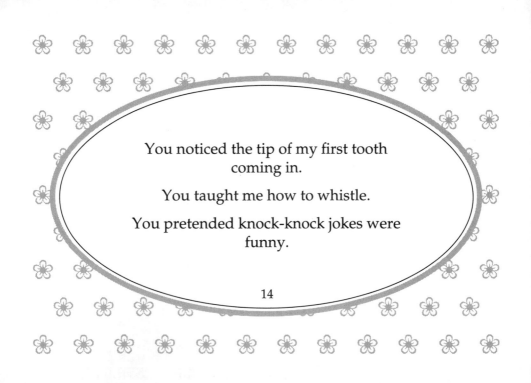

You noticed the tip of my first tooth coming in.

You taught me how to whistle.

You pretended knock-knock jokes were funny.

14

I didn't cry on the first day of school, but you did.

You made me my first Halloween costume.

15

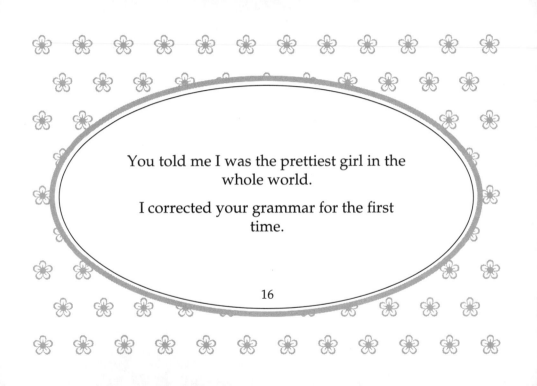

You told me I was the prettiest girl in the whole world.

I corrected your grammar for the first time.

16

You told me you drove around for hours
because I'd only nap
in the car.

We munched our way through the
supermarket.

The orthodontist gave you the bad news.

We couldn't stop giggling.

I thought the potty you brought home was a new hat.

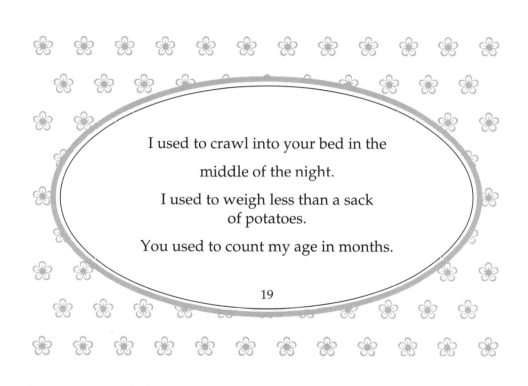

I used to crawl into your bed in the
middle of the night.

I used to weigh less than a sack
of potatoes.

You used to count my age in months.

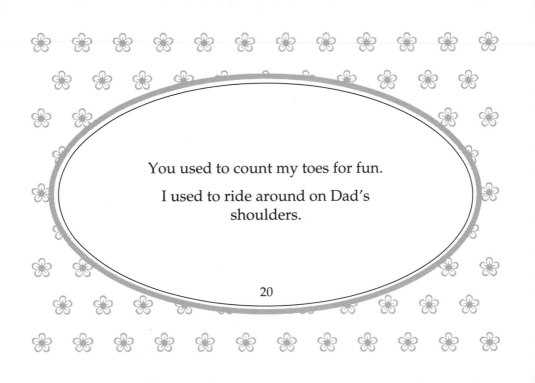

You used to count my toes for fun.

I used to ride around on Dad's shoulders.

20

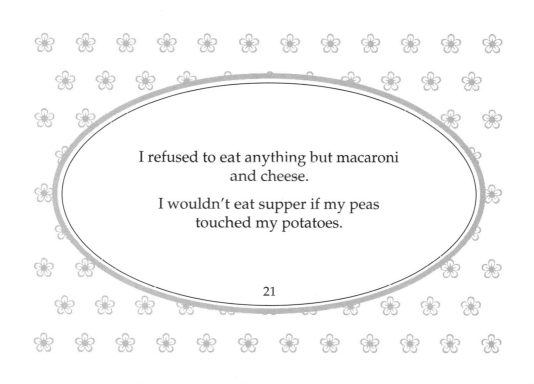

I refused to eat anything but macaroni and cheese.

I wouldn't eat supper if my peas touched my potatoes.

I actually liked it when you took my
picture.

I begged to go meet Santa.

(You took me to meet Santa and I cried.)

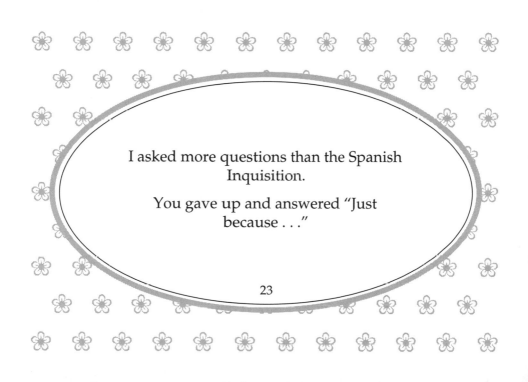

I asked more questions than the Spanish Inquisition.

You gave up and answered "Just because . . ."

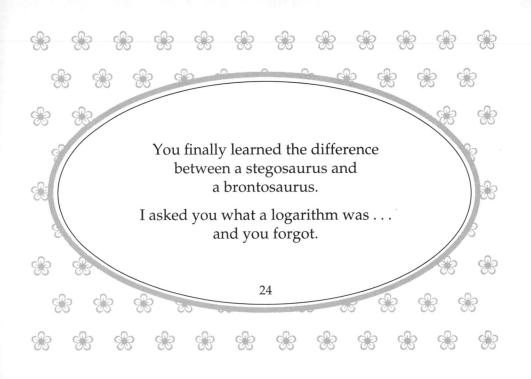

You finally learned the difference
between a stegosaurus and
a brontosaurus.

I asked you what a logarithm was . . .
and you forgot.

24

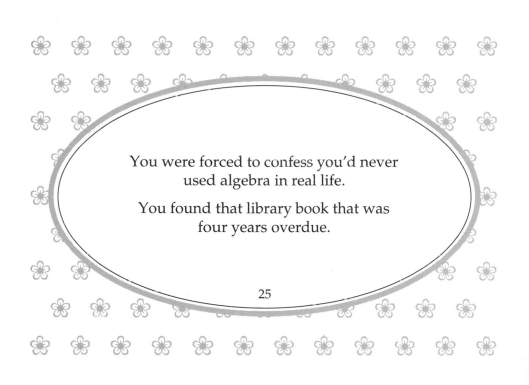

You were forced to confess you'd never used algebra in real life.

You found that library book that was four years overdue.

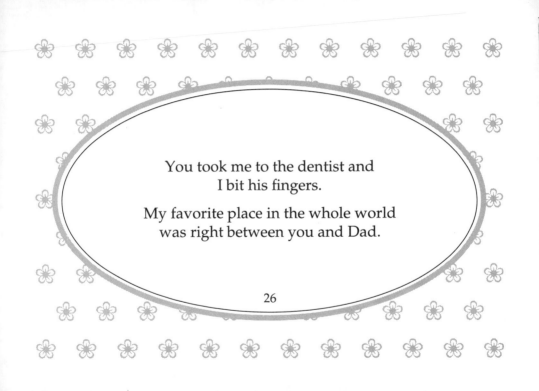

You took me to the dentist and
I bit his fingers.

My favorite place in the whole world
was right between you and Dad.

26

You had to turn back from a trip to get my stuffed animal.

I beat you at chess and you weren't even trying to lose.

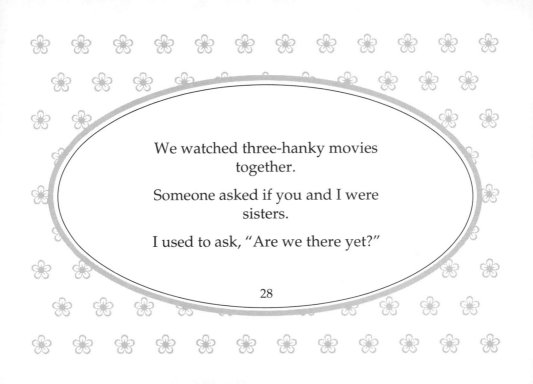

We watched three-hanky movies together.

Someone asked if you and I were sisters.

I used to ask, "Are we there yet?"

28

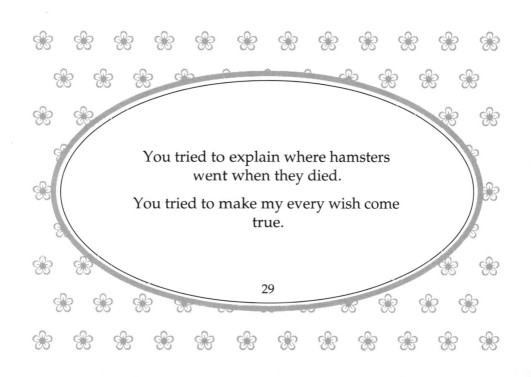

You tried to explain where hamsters went when they died.

You tried to make my every wish come true.

29

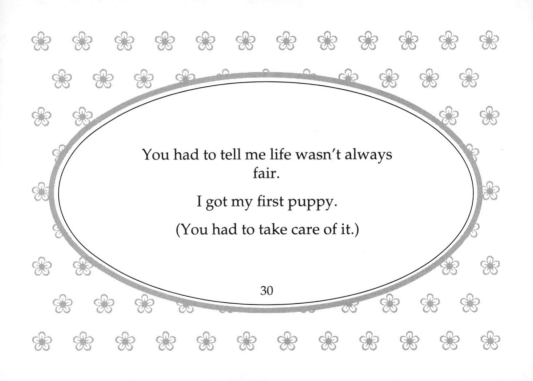

You had to tell me life wasn't always fair.

I got my first puppy.

(You had to take care of it.)

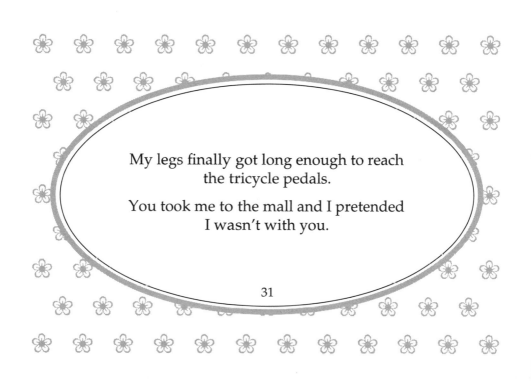

My legs finally got long enough to reach the tricycle pedals.

You took me to the mall and I pretended I wasn't with you.

31

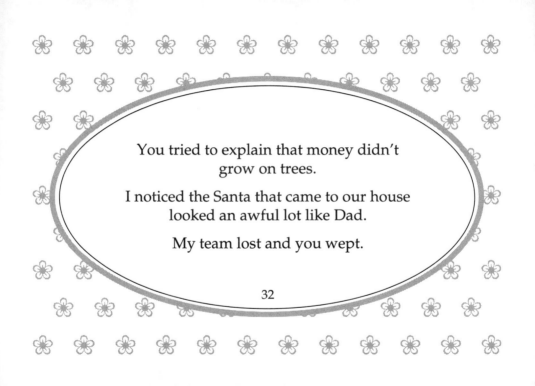

You tried to explain that money didn't grow on trees.

I noticed the Santa that came to our house looked an awful lot like Dad.

My team lost and you wept.

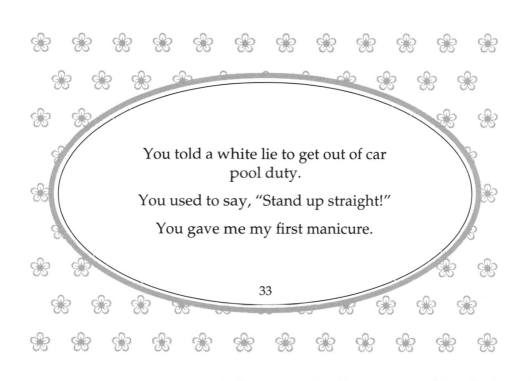

You told a white lie to get out of car pool duty.

You used to say, "Stand up straight!"

You gave me my first manicure.

33

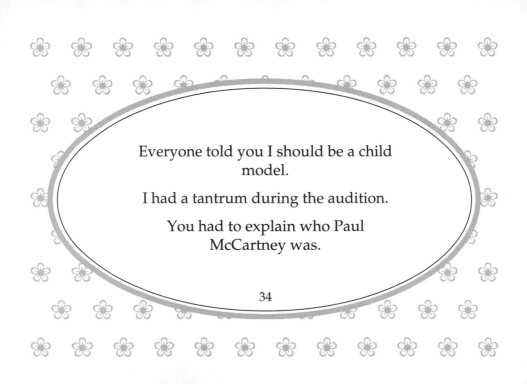

Everyone told you I should be a child model.

I had a tantrum during the audition.

You had to explain who Paul McCartney was.

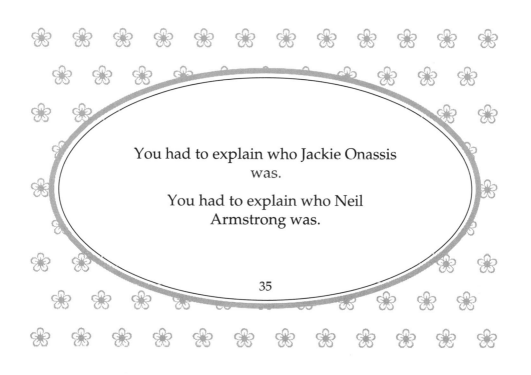

You had to explain who Jackie Onassis was.

You had to explain who Neil Armstrong was.

I couldn't believe you were once a kid yourself.

You got to play with my Barbie dolls.

We cooked Thanksgiving dinner together.

You stayed up all night wrapping
Christmas presents.

You stood in the rain while I marched in
a parade.

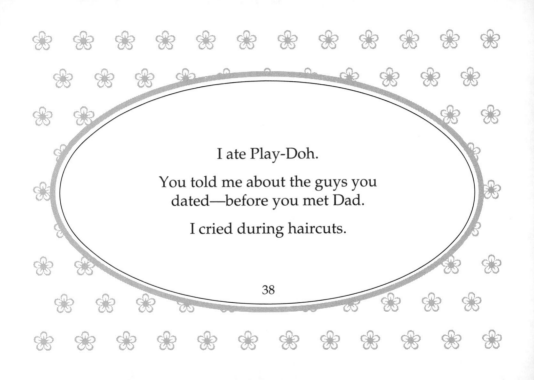

I ate Play-Doh.

You told me about the guys you dated—before you met Dad.

I cried during haircuts.

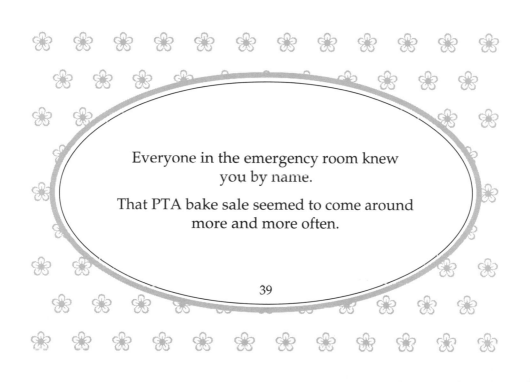

Everyone in the emergency room knew
you by name.

That PTA bake sale seemed to come around
more and more often.

39

You and Dad took us camping and pitched the tent in poison sumac.

You said something was "cool" and I groaned.

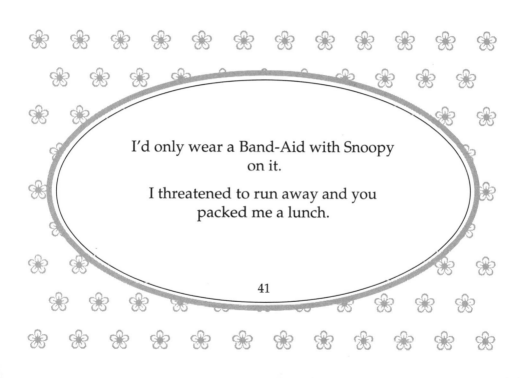

I'd only wear a Band-Aid with Snoopy on it.

I threatened to run away and you packed me a lunch.

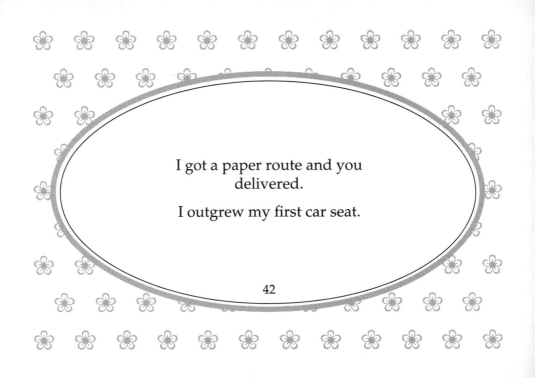

I got a paper route and you delivered.

I outgrew my first car seat.

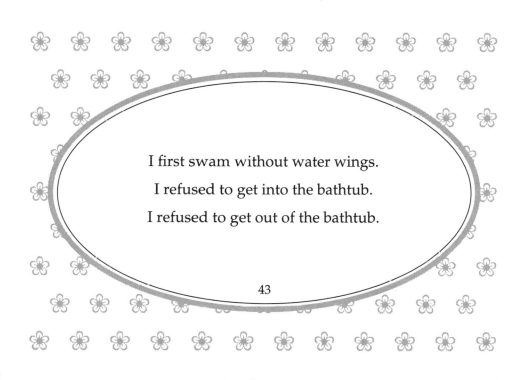

I first swam without water wings.

I refused to get into the bathtub.

I refused to get out of the bathtub.

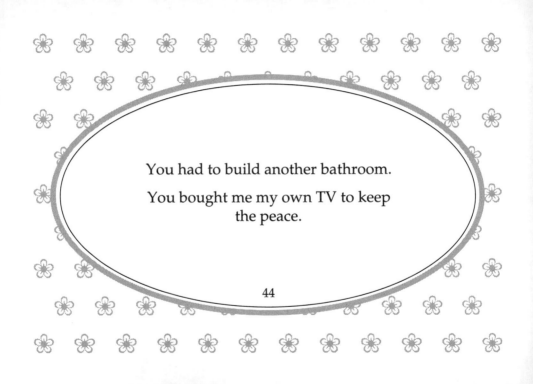

You had to build another bathroom.

You bought me my own TV to keep
the peace.

44

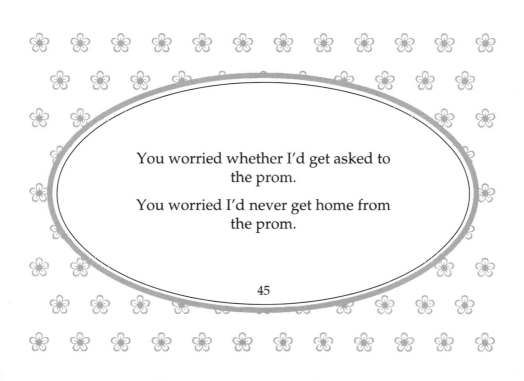

You worried whether I'd get asked to the prom.

You worried I'd never get home from the prom.

45

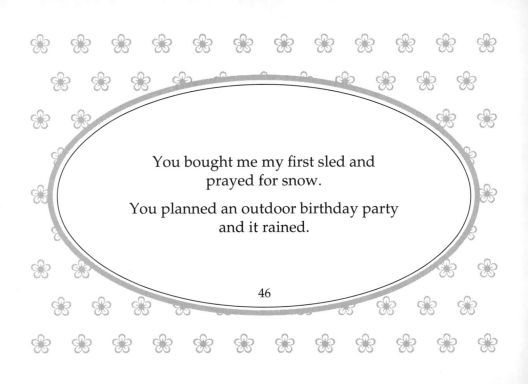

You bought me my first sled and prayed for snow.

You planned an outdoor birthday party and it rained.

46

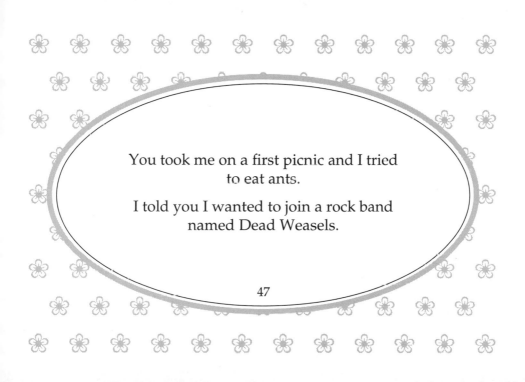

You took me on a first picnic and I tried to eat ants.

I told you I wanted to join a rock band named Dead Weasels.

47

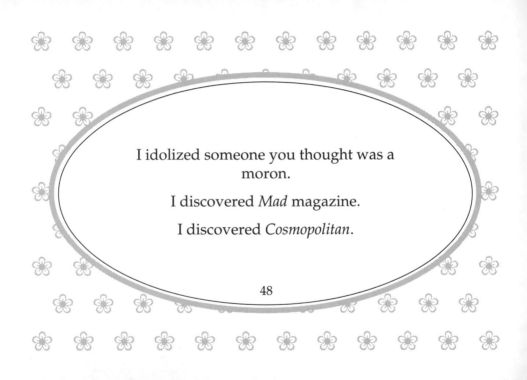

I idolized someone you thought was a moron.

I discovered *Mad* magazine.

I discovered *Cosmopolitan*.

You left me home alone for the first
time and I actually didn't burn
the house down.

I convinced the babysitter we always
had ice cream for supper.

49

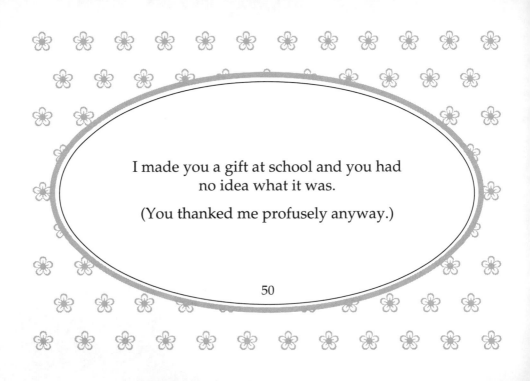

I made you a gift at school and you had
no idea what it was.

(You thanked me profusely anyway.)

You bought me my own phone.

You got the phone bill.

I played a cabbage in the school spring pageant.

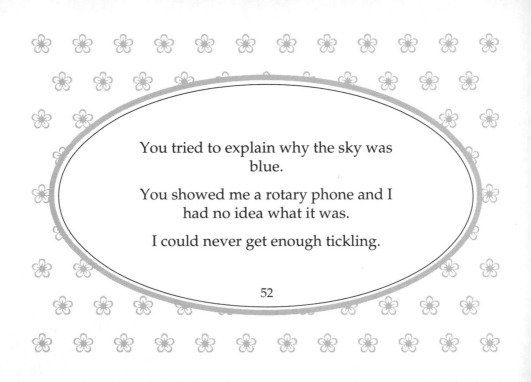

You tried to explain why the sky was blue.

You showed me a rotary phone and I had no idea what it was.

I could never get enough tickling.

52

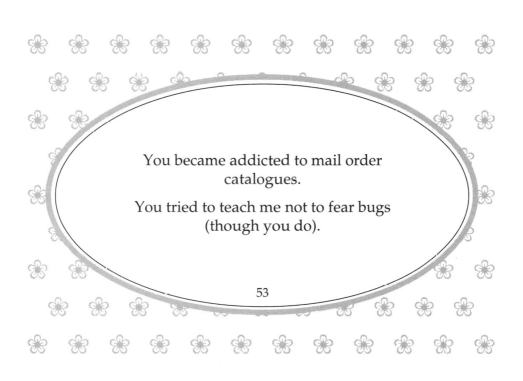

You became addicted to mail order catalogues.

You tried to teach me not to fear bugs (though you do).

53

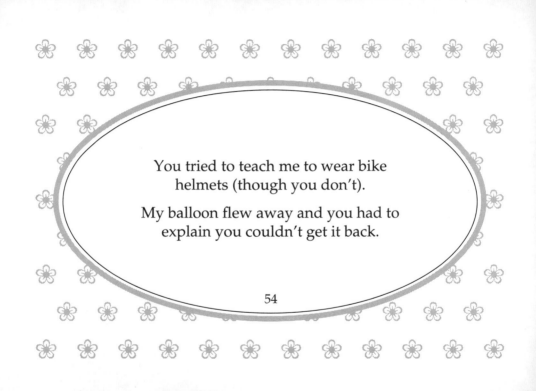

You tried to teach me to wear bike helmets (though you don't).

My balloon flew away and you had to explain you couldn't get it back.

54

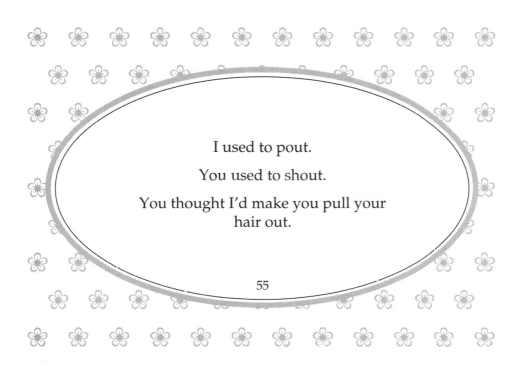

I used to pout.

You used to shout.

You thought I'd make you pull your
hair out.

55

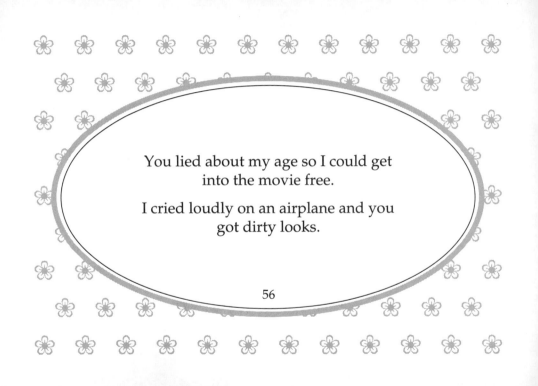

You lied about my age so I could get into the movie free.

I cried loudly on an airplane and you got dirty looks.

56

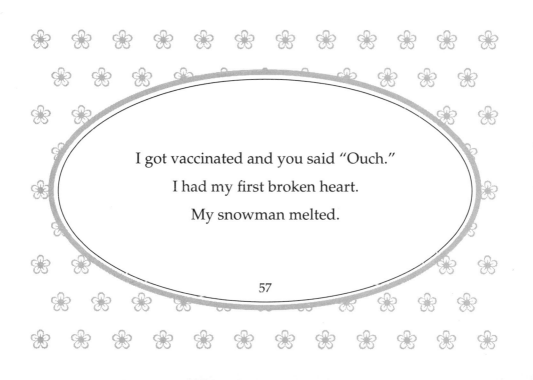

I got vaccinated and you said "Ouch."

I had my first broken heart.

My snowman melted.

57

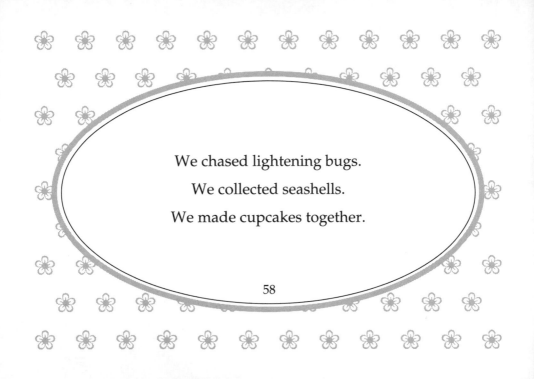

We chased lightening bugs.

We collected seashells.

We made cupcakes together.

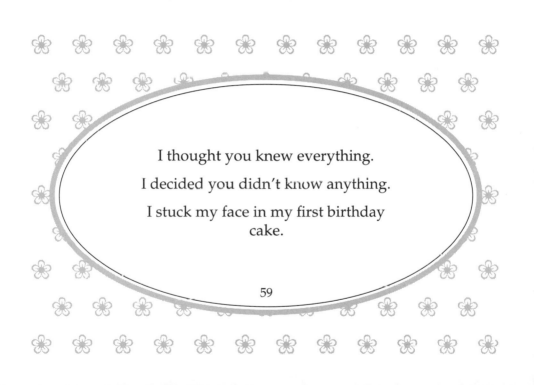

I thought you knew everything.

I decided you didn't know anything.

I stuck my face in my first birthday cake.

Everyone said I looked just like you.

Everyone said I looked just like Dad.

I got stood up for a date and you wept.

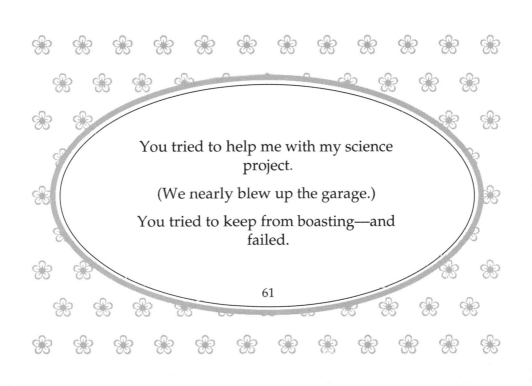

You tried to help me with my science project.

(We nearly blew up the garage.)

You tried to keep from boasting—and failed.

61

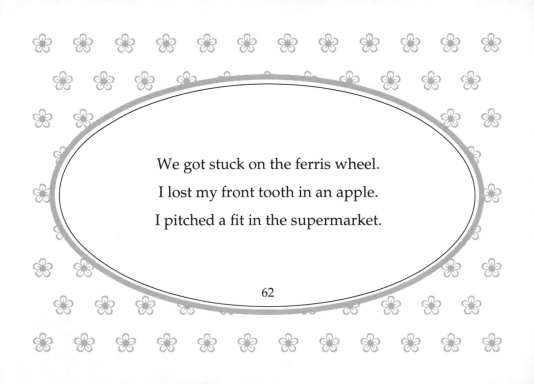

We got stuck on the ferris wheel.

I lost my front tooth in an apple.

I pitched a fit in the supermarket.

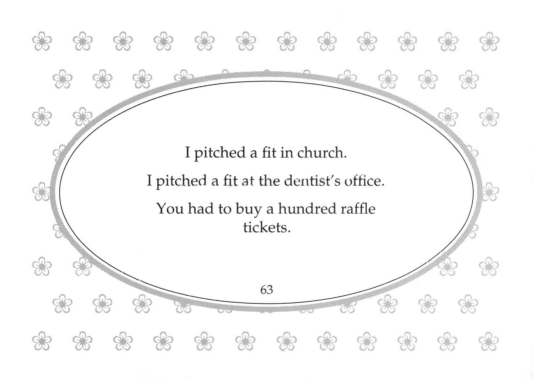

I pitched a fit in church.

I pitched a fit at the dentist's office.

You had to buy a hundred raffle tickets.

63

You had to buy eight dozen boxes of cookies.

I graduated preschool.

I talked you into adopting a Cabbage Patch doll.

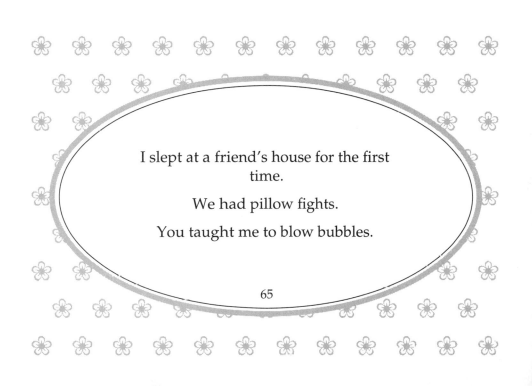

I slept at a friend's house for the first time.

We had pillow fights.

You taught me to blow bubbles.

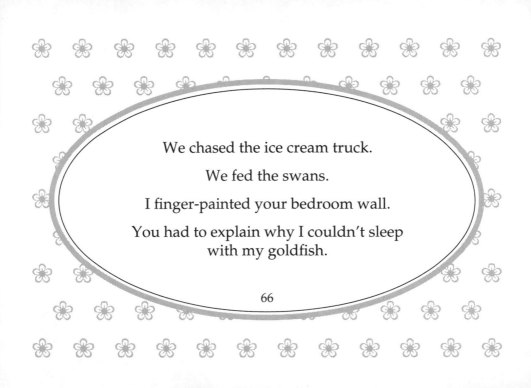

We chased the ice cream truck.

We fed the swans.

I finger-painted your bedroom wall.

You had to explain why I couldn't sleep
with my goldfish.

You took me back-to-school shopping.

We jumped in the autumn leaves.

We survived that winter with 29 snow days.

I went through my "awkward" phase.

I got stung by a bee.

I got spooked by a monster under the bed.

A bully picked on me and you called the bully's mother.

You tried setting curfews.

You lectured me and my eyes glazed over.

All I needed to have fun was
imagination.

I made plans to live in my tree-house
full time.

You knew by heart where every bathroom
in town was.

I took my first train ride.

71

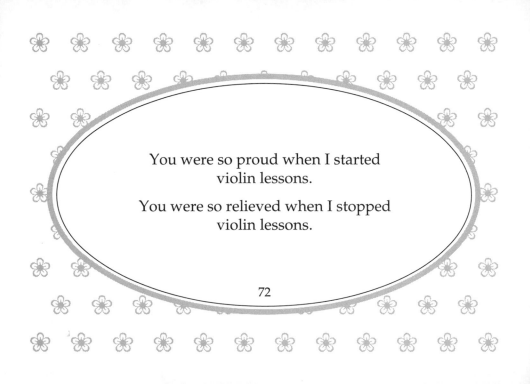

You were so proud when I started
violin lessons.

You were so relieved when I stopped
violin lessons.

72

I ate gummy worms.

I started to prefer my friends to you.

All I wanted from you was a hug.

73

I buried you in the sand.

I bit off the bottom of the ice cream cone.

I discovered the salt and pepper shakers.

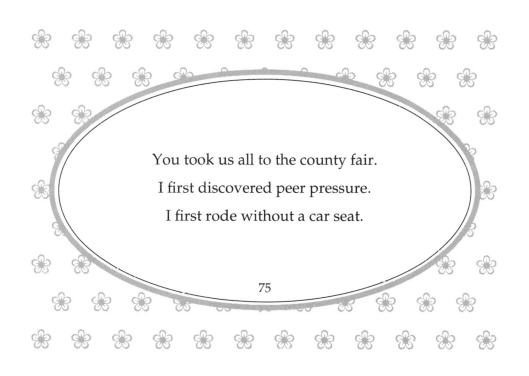

You took us all to the county fair.

I first discovered peer pressure.

I first rode without a car seat.

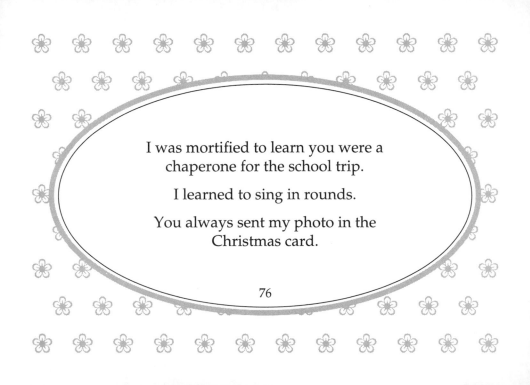

I was mortified to learn you were a chaperone for the school trip.

I learned to sing in rounds.

You always sent my photo in the Christmas card.

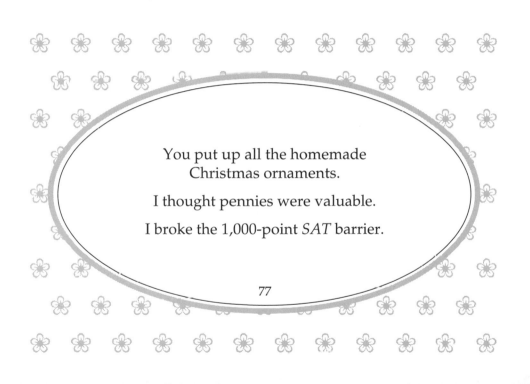

You put up all the homemade
Christmas ornaments.

I thought pennies were valuable.

I broke the 1,000-point *SAT* barrier.

77

You couldn't figure out my homework assignment.

I wept because my gym uniform was so ugly.

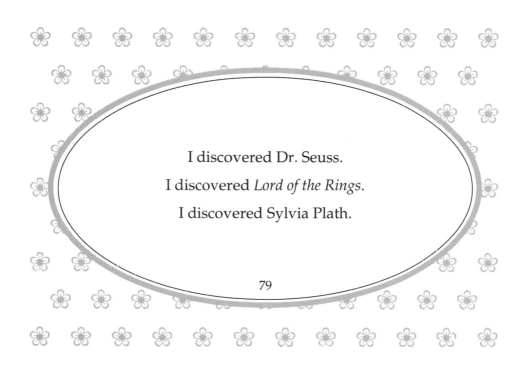

I discovered Dr. Seuss.

I discovered *Lord of the Rings*.

I discovered Sylvia Plath.

I wanted to paint my bedroom black.

I started to write bad poetry.

I realized you weren't fearless.

I discovered there was money in your purse.

I used to go "exploring" in your closets.

All the phone calls started to be for me.

All the invitations started to be for me.

81

I had to pee as soon as we left the rest stop.

Watching *Bambi* scared me silly.

You helped me carve jack-o-lanterns.

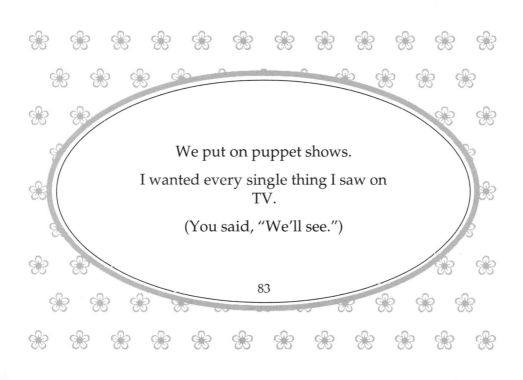

We put on puppet shows.

I wanted every single thing I saw on TV.

(You said, "We'll see.")

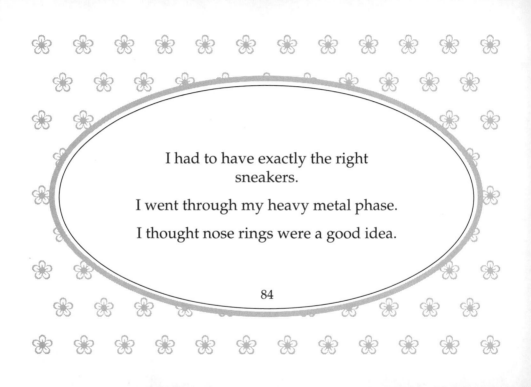

I had to have exactly the right sneakers.

I went through my heavy metal phase.

I thought nose rings were a good idea.

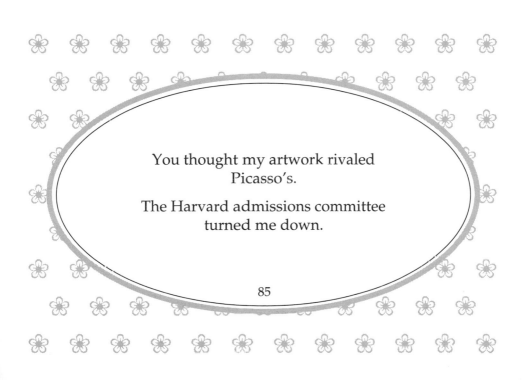

You thought my artwork rivaled Picasso's.

The Harvard admissions committee turned me down.

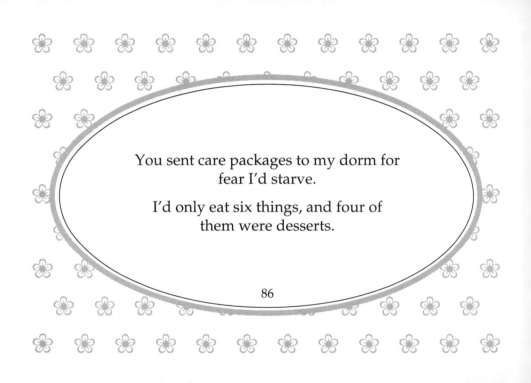

You sent care packages to my dorm for fear I'd starve.

I'd only eat six things, and four of them were desserts.

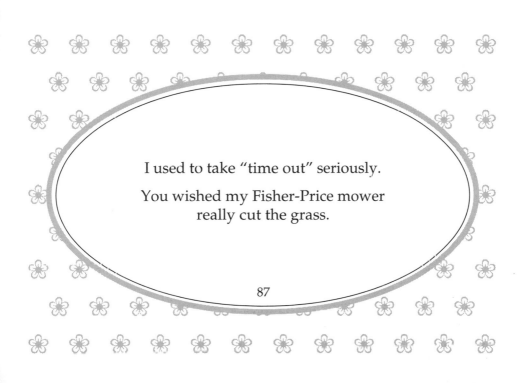

I used to take "time out" seriously.

You wished my Fisher-Price mower
really cut the grass.

87

I tottered around in your high heels.

I begged you to let me shave my legs.

I stuck out my chest and pretended I had "bosoms."

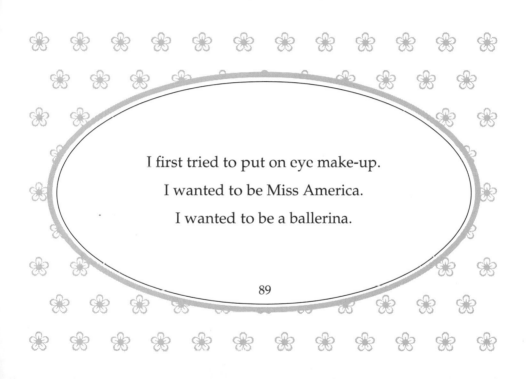

I first tried to put on eye make-up.

I wanted to be Miss America.

I wanted to be a ballerina.

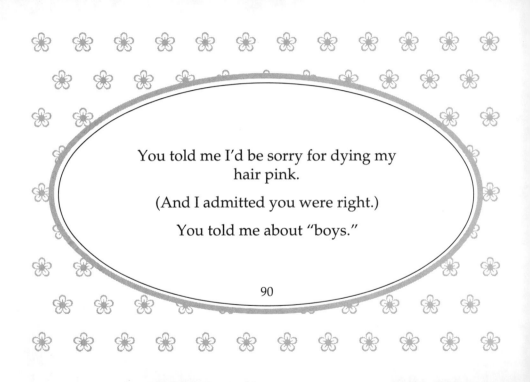

You told me I'd be sorry for dying my hair pink.

(And I admitted you were right.)

You told me about "boys."

We discovered we both had a crush on Mel Gibson.

We held each other at Grandma's funeral.

You took me for my first pair of high heels.

I cooked dinner for you and Dad in my first apartment.

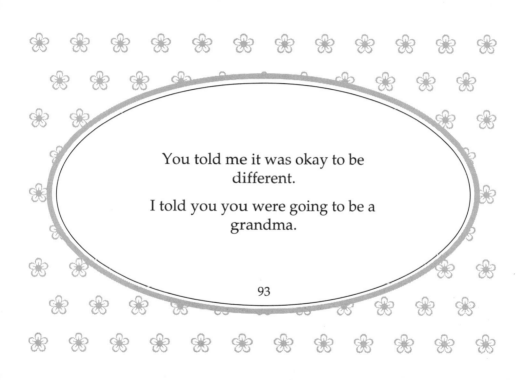

You told me it was okay to be different.

I told you you were going to be a grandma.

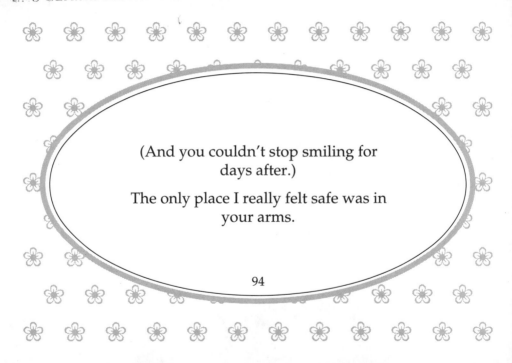

(And you couldn't stop smiling for
days after.)

The only place I really felt safe was in
your arms.

94